HIGHER LOVE

Discovering God's Design for Your Marriage

LEADER'S GUIDE

FOCUS ON THE FAMILY

TYNDALE HOUSE PUBLISHERS, INC.
Carol Stream, Illinois

Essentials of Marriage: Higher Love
Leader's Guide

Focus on the Family and the accompanying logo and design are federally registered trademarks of
Focus on the Family, Colorado Springs, CO 80995.

A Focus on the Family book published by Tyndale House Publishers, Carol Stream, Illinois 60188

TYNDALE is a registered trademark of Tyndale House Publishers, Inc. Tyndale's quill logo is a trademark of Tyndale House Publishers, Inc.

ISBN: 978-1-58997-583-5

Printed in the United States of America
1 2 3 4 5 6 7 / 15 14 13 12 11 10 09

CONTENTS

WELCOME!

Marriage can be tough—but learning about it doesn't have to be. In fact, we think you'll find this course easy to use, to the point—even fun.

At the heart of each session is a DVD presentation featuring some of today's top marriage experts.

Then there's the Participant's Guide—the book each of your group members will need to make the course personal.

Finally, there's the Leader's Guide—the book you're holding right now. It's designed to help you turn the DVD and Participant's Guide into a lively group experience in which spouses learn and support each other.

Preparing for the Session

Before each meeting, review the session plan in this book. Look at the corresponding chapter in the Participant's Guide. Preview the DVD segment if possible; then make sure it's cued up for your group to watch.

For most sessions, you'll need pencils or pens. For some, if your group is large, you may need chalkboard and chalk or other display surface and writing tool (newsprint and marker, white board and marker, etc.). You may also need to gather a few other easy-to-find materials, listed in "Setting the Stage" at the start of each session.

Leading the Session

You'll find the session plans easy to follow. Instructions to you are in regular type; things you might say to the group are in bold type; suggested answers are in parentheses.

Each session, designed to last about an hour, includes five steps:

1. Getting Together (5 minutes)
Using a game or other "icebreaker" activity, you'll grab the group's interest and build a sense of community. This step is optional; if your group members need help getting acquainted, or if they just like to have a good time, it can be especially valuable.

2. Finding Yourself (5-10 minutes)
Participants take a survey to help them see how this session topic might benefit them.

3. Catching the Vision (20-25 minutes)
Watch and discuss the DVD segment.

4. Digging Deeper (10 minutes)
If part of your group's mission is discussing God's Word, you'll want to include this Bible study step. If yours is more of a community outreach effort, you may wish to condense or delete this section.

5. Making It Work (10 minutes)
It's time for practical application, as group members use the corresponding section of the Participant's Guide to come up with action plans for their own marriages.

6. Bringing It Home (5 minutes)
For you, this is a brief wrap-up. For group members, it's something to read later: practical advice from a counselor.

Tips for Success

- If your group is like most, you often run out of time before you run out of discussion questions and activities. What to do? Simply choose the exercises and questions you think will be most helpful to your group and concentrate on those. Try starting with the bare essentials—watching the DVD and applying the principles through the "Making It Work" activity—and add steps as your schedule allows.
- Invite discussion, but don't be surprised if some group members are reluctant to share personal information. If people want to reflect silently on a probing question, encourage them to do so.
- Couples will benefit most, of course, if both spouses attend your sessions. In some cases, though, schedules or interest levels may require some spouses to attend alone. If that's true in your group, be sure to help these individuals feel welcomed and supported. You'll need to adapt some activities in this guide accordingly. Instead of having spouses discuss a question, for example,

you may want to form subgroups of three to five—or simply skip questions that would be too personal for individuals to discuss with anyone other than a mate.

- Don't allow laughter at anyone's expense. If some of the discussion questions seem likely to cause embarrassment, feel free to omit them; if they would be more appropriately answered between husband and wife in private, encourage group members to do so later.

- Instead of pressing group members to reveal information they're not comfortable sharing, tell an occasional story on yourself if you like. Propose the following guidelines to participants: Before raising a question or referring to an experience, make sure it won't embarrass your spouse; if in doubt, privately ask your spouse's permission beforehand; maintain confidentiality.

- Let participants know that if they're struggling in their marriages, help is available. Provide contact information for local Christian counselors, especially any who are connected with your church. If your church staff doesn't know of a therapist, Focus on the Family has a referral network of Christian counselors. For information, call 1-800-A-FAMILY and ask for the counseling department. You can also download free, printable brochures offering help for couples at http://www.focusonthefamily.com/marriage/articles/brochures.aspx.

- If possible, each group member—not just each couple—should have a Participant's Guide. Otherwise, spouses won't be able to write individual responses to opinion questions. It's a good idea to have a few extra copies of the Participant's Guide on hand, so that visitors (and those who forgot their books) can take part.

- If you don't have an answer to every question, join the club! It's okay to say, "I don't know." Ask group members to share wisdom from their experience. Refer people to books like *Complete Guide to the First Five Years of Marriage* (Focus on the Family/Tyndale House, 2006), which contains help for almost any stage of married life.

- Have a good time! Marriage may be serious business, but most of your group members probably would appreciate a light touch as they learn. Let your group be a place where spouses can laugh together and gain perspective on their marital challenges.

- Pray. Pray for your group members during the week. Urge them to pray for each other. Ask God to help each person become the loving, effective mate he or she was meant to be.

For additional tips on leading your group, see the "Instructions for Leaders" feature on the DVD. You can also find further advice for your couples at focusonthefamily.com/marriage.

Ready to have a lasting, positive impact on the marriages represented in your group? May God bless you as you lead!

Note: Many issues addressed in this series are difficult ones. Some couples may need to address them in greater detail and depth. The DVD presentations and this guide are intended as general advice only, and not to replace clinical counseling, medical treatment, legal counsel, or financial guidance.

FINDING HOLINESS AND HAPPINESS

Why did God invent marriage? To make us happy? Not according to author Gary Thomas, whose ideas about wedded bliss in this DVD segment may turn your assumptions upside-down.

God is more interested in making us *holy*, Gary explains, and marriage is a great place to work on that. As if that's not enough, Gary urges husbands and wives to see God not only as their Father—but also their Father-in-law. That's because our spouses are God's children, and we're to treat them that way.

Host Dr. Greg Smalley adds a story from his own marriage, rounding out a thought-provoking look at why you got married—even if you didn't know it at the time.

Session Aim
To help spouses see their marriages as opportunities for spiritual growth, and to welcome trials that might otherwise frustrate them.

Setting the Stage
- Read this session plan and Chapter 1 in the Participant's Guide.
- Provide pencils or pens.
- If you want to use the "Point of View" icebreaker in Step 1, photocopy and cut out the drawings (one copy per couple).
- Cue up the DVD to segment 1, "Finding Holiness and Happiness."

1. GETTING TOGETHER

Optional Icebreaker
(5 minutes)

If you'd like to start on a light note, try this activity. Before the session, photocopy the following "Point of View" pictures. Cut the "Point of View 1" and "Point of View 2" diagrams apart.

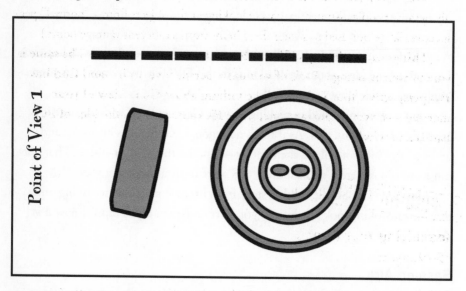

As people arrive, give each couple a copy of "Point of View 1."

Let couples try to decide what's depicted. When it's time to begin your meeting, ask whether anyone's figured out what the pictures represent. (They are, in order, the letters of the word *MARRIAGE*, a wedding ring, and a wedding cake—all viewed from above.)

In case people doubt your explanation of the drawings, pass out copies of "Point of View 2." Then say something like this:

Why was it hard to tell what the first set of pictures represented? (Probably because people assumed they were looking at the objects from a "normal" perspective. We're not used to seeing these items from a different vantage point.)

Things can look very different from another point of view. The same is true of your marriage. Each of you has a perspective on it—and God has His perspective, too. Today we'll be talking about God's view of your marriage—a very important one, since He came up with the idea of husbands and wives.

2. FINDING YOURSELF

Identifying Your Needs
(5-10 minutes)

Ask group members to turn to the "Finding Yourself" section in the Participant's Guide. Invite them to fill out the survey; couples can work together or individually. Then let volunteers share a few of their answers with the group.

1. **How might each of the following describe your wedding in 10 words or less? Why?**

   your maid of honor _____

   your best man _____

   your parents _____

   your pastor _____

   God _____

   (Answers will vary; a best man might fondly remember tying the groom's shoelaces together before he stumbled down the aisle, while parents could see it as the day their "empty nest" syndrome officially began. The important thing is to see how perspectives differ, and to start thinking about what God's view of a particular marriage might be.)

2. **How would you rank the following elements of marriage from most important to least? How do you think God would rank these factors? If the rankings are different, what do you think accounts for that?**
   ___ whether spouses agree on political issues
   ___ how often spouses pray together
   ___ whether spouses plan to have children
   ___ how involved spouses are in ministry
   ___ how much spouses enjoy each other's company
   ___ how much money spouses give to church work

(Rankings will differ. Participants may assume God cares mainly about the "spiritual" issues—praying together, ministry, and church giving. But there's no reason to assume He doesn't care about the rest, too.)

3. **How do you think each of the following would define marriage?**
   your spouse _____
   Jesus Christ _____
   someone who's been married a dozen times _____
   your kids, if you have any _____
   your oldest living relative _____

(Answers may vary widely. Pay special attention to people's ideas about what Jesus might say. If time allows, ask them to explain their replies.)

4. **Did your wedding ceremony acknowledge God's involvement in your marriage? If so, how? If not, why not?** _____

_____

(Those married in a church probably heard words about God, whether or not they took His involvement seriously. A traditional ceremony usually includes statements about being gathered in the presence of God, and not separating what God has joined.)

5. Since your wedding, have you acknowledged God's involvement in your marriage? If so, how? If not, why not? _____

_____

(Some couples may have prayed together, though many might have a hard time coming up with specific examples of recognizing God's role.)

Watching and Discussing the DVD
(20-25 minutes)

After viewing the DVD, use questions like these to help group members think through what they saw and heard.

1. If you stood on a street corner in your town and asked people, "Why did God invent marriage?" what would they answer? If you surveyed 100 of those people, how many do you think would give you replies like each of the following? Why?
   - "For raising children."
   - "So we wouldn't be lonely."
   - "To torture us."
   - "To make us better people."
   - "Who said He invented marriage?"

(Opinions will differ. If time allows, ask participants which of the replies would come closest to their own.)

2. Gary Thomas believes God created marriage to make us holy, not just to make us happy. Which of the following best describes your reaction to that idea?
   - "That figures, since God doesn't want anyone to be happy."
   - "It doesn't seem to be working."
   - "Being happy is a result of being holy."

- **"That explains why I'm so miserable."**
- **other** _____

(Some participants probably will see the third choice as the "right" answer, but encourage people to be honest in their responses.)

3. **How was Gary's experience with the ice trays an example of a spiritual challenge in marriage? What do you think God wanted him to do in that situation? Why?**

(It's hard to go against the grain of your personality, habits, and upbringing. For Gary to adjust to his wife's preference rather than insisting on his own would require the kind of unselfishness, love, and empathy that God calls us to—and develops in us as we become more like His Son.)

4. **Who's one of the holiest people you've ever met? Was he or she also one of the happiest? Does that make you interested in holiness? Why or why not?**

(If participants think of "holy" people as overly serious or sour, they probably aren't interested in holiness. Since true holiness refers to being set apart for God's use, a "holy" person could have a bubbly personality or a somber one; neither of those is a guarantee of happiness. The bottom line is that many of us don't really understand holiness *or* happiness.)

5. **What do you think you could learn about loving, giving, forgiving, confronting, or asking forgiveness in each of the following situations?**
   - **Your spouse blames you when the restaurant you chose for dinner has a long waiting list.**
   - **You borrow your spouse's cell phone and discover that he or she's been getting calls from an old flame.**
   - **Your spouse can't seem to give up smoking, and you have asthma.**

(Being unjustly blamed could give you a chance to express love by forgiving your spouse; feeling betrayed could teach you how to confront in a loving way, and to give your mate the benefit of the doubt instead of jumping to conclusions; living with a mate who endangers your health could show you the value of confronting and giving the support needed to help the person stop smoking.)

6. **Gary says that many people expect their spouses to give them fulfillment, joy, and unconditional love—which only God can provide reliably. If you gave up those expectations tomorrow morning, how might the rest of your week be different?**

   (It might free you to love your spouse without insisting on anything in return; it could motivate you to build a closer relationship with God.)

7. **If you really believe your spouse is God's child, and that He's protective of him or her, how will it affect what you do in the following situations?**
   - **You wish your spouse would lose 20 pounds.**
   - **Your spouse forgets to pay the car insurance bill, then gets in a fender bender after coverage lapses.**
   - **Your spouse is accused of shoplifting.**

   (Answers will vary. But you'd probably be more gentle with your spouse. You'd be slower to accuse or blame. You'd be more likely to trust God to bring about any needed changes in your mate instead of trying to make them yourself or berating your spouse for changing too slowly.)

8. **According to Gary, we need to accept the following three spiritual realities about marriage. Which of them is hardest for you to understand? To accept? To remember during everyday disappointments and conflicts?**
   - **Marriage is a very difficult relationship.**
   - **You stay married even though your spouse isn't perfect.**
   - **God is your spiritual Father-in-law, and you love your spouse out of reverence for Him.**

   (Replies will differ. Some group members may not have thought much about these concepts; be patient if they aren't ready to answer yet.)

9. **Why does Gary sometimes pray when he wakes up about loving his wife more than anyone else does? How would you put that message in the form of a prayer about your spouse? How often would you be willing to pray it?**

   (Gary's prayer may remind him that he's the only husband his wife has, which gives him a unique responsibility to show love to her. Group members' versions of the prayer will vary, as will their interest in praying it. If time allows, ask participants what effect they think the prayer might have.)

Bible Study
(10 minutes)

If your group has been organized with Bible study in mind, have volunteers read these passages and discuss the questions that follow them.

> The LORD God said, "It is not good for the man to be alone. I will make a helper suitable for him." . . .
>
> So the man gave names to all the livestock, the birds of the air and all the beasts of the field.
>
> But for Adam no suitable helper was found. So the LORD God caused the man to fall into a deep sleep; and while he was sleeping, he took one of the man's ribs and closed up the place with flesh. Then the LORD God made a woman from the rib he had taken out of the man, and he brought her to the man.
>
> The man said,
> "This is now bone of my bones
> and flesh of my flesh;
> she shall be called 'woman,'
> for she was taken out of man."
>
> For this reason a man will leave his father and mother and be united to his wife, and they will become one flesh.
>
> The man and his wife were both naked, and they felt no shame. *(Genesis 2:18, 20-25)*

1. **Do you think God expected to find a "suitable helper" for Adam in the animal kingdom? Why or why not?**
   (No; He declared His intention to make one before the "search" was conducted. Perhaps the search was for Adam's benefit, since God already knew the kind of companion Adam needed.)

2. **Why do you suppose God took Eve out of Adam, only to decree that they reunite? What does this tell you about God's purposes for marriage?**
(Answers will vary. Many have suggested that the symbolism of "two from one" and "two becoming one" echoes God's three-in-one nature. It might also echo the oneness and care for each other's bodies [Ephesians 5:28] that He wants married couples to have.)

3. **Is it hard to imagine feeling "no shame" about being naked? Why or why not? Do you think that's still true of most husbands and wives? Why or why not?**
(If feeling no shame were common after the Fall, the writer probably wouldn't have mentioned the issue. Part of a healthy marriage involves learning to enjoy each other's bodies, but spouses often continue to struggle with embarrassment or a lack of confidence about their appearance.)

4. **If Genesis 2:18, 20-25 were the only thing you knew about men and women, how would you describe God's view of marriage?**
(Some possibilities: God cares whether people are alone; the companionship and teamwork of marriage are designed to meet a human need; sexuality [man and woman becoming "one flesh"] is basic to that relationship.)

> When Jesus had finished saying these things, he left Galilee and went into the region of Judea to the other side of the Jordan. Large crowds followed him, and he healed them there.
>
> Some Pharisees came to him to test him. They asked, "Is it lawful for a man to divorce his wife for any and every reason?"
>
> "Haven't you read," he replied, "that at the beginning the Creator 'made them male and female,' and said, 'For this reason a man will leave his father and mother and be united to his wife, and the two will become one flesh'? So they are no longer two, but one. Therefore what God has joined together, let man not separate."
>
> "Why then," they asked, "did Moses command that a man give his wife a certificate of divorce and send her away?"
>
> Jesus replied, "Moses permitted you to divorce your wives because your hearts were hard. But it was not this way from the beginning. I tell you that anyone who divorces his wife, except for marital unfaithfulness, and marries another woman commits adultery."

The disciples said to him, "If this is the situation between a husband and wife, it is better not to marry."

Jesus replied, "Not everyone can accept this word, but only those to whom it has been given. For some are eunuchs because they were born that way; others were made that way by men; and others have renounced marriage because of the kingdom of heaven. The one who can accept this should accept it." (Matthew 19:1-12)

5. **Is it lawful today to divorce "for any and every reason"? What reasons do divorcing couples tend to give?**

    (In most of Western culture, legal grounds for divorce are broad enough that they can be made to apply in almost any situation. Reasons like "incompatibility" and "alienation of affection" are cited in court; divorced couples often say they "just drifted apart," "outgrew each other," "couldn't communicate," or that one partner was "emotionally unavailable." In other cases, of course, more specific reasons like infidelity or abuse are involved.)

6. **Why did the disciples think Jesus' view of marriage made singleness look good? Do you think most people would agree? Why or why not?**

    (The disciples appeared to want more options than Jesus was giving them. Many people today would, too, though they might prefer "serial monogamy" to singleness.)

7. **If Matthew 19:1-12 were the only thing you knew about men and women, how would you describe God's view of marriage?**

    (Some possibilities: Marriage is meant to last for life; God joins spouses together; marriage is desirable, but not for everyone.)

8. **If you believe that God Himself has joined you and your spouse together, how might this affect your reactions to the following situations?**
    - **You disagree strongly over whether to buy a house.**
    - **You're tired of spending holidays with your in-laws.**
    - **Your spouse is diagnosed with Alzheimer's.**
    - **The two of you are asked to start a small group for your church.**
    - **Your spouse warns that the two of you are "drifting apart."**

(Believing this might make you more willing to give up your "rights" in order to stay together. If both of you believe it, you might also be more willing to jump into conflict resolution without fear that your spouse will leave if he or she doesn't get his or her way. You could be more likely to stay with your declining spouse or start a small group because you believe it's part of God's purpose in bringing you together. You probably would do all you could to avoid drifting apart.)

Applying the Principles
(10 minutes)

Have the group turn to the "Making It Work" section in the Participant's Guide. Allow at least five minutes for couples to work through the "Happiness and Holiness Meals" exercise. Then let them share the results with fellow participants.

To help couples apply what they learned, try questions like the following.

Which foods did you connect with holiness? Which ones with happiness? Why?

(There are no "right" answers here. The goal is to help group members think about their preconceptions.)

Did anyone come up with a meal that's both "holy" and "happy"?

(If anyone did, ask for "nutrition information" on the percentages of holiness and happiness. As needed, emphasize that we can have a heart of both happiness and holiness.)

If a person believes holiness is all about deprivation and suffering and unpleasantness, how will he or she react to the idea that God wants us to be holy, not just happy?

(Probably by ignoring God's view.)

If you think happiness is all about comfort and pleasure and getting your own way, how will you respond to Gary Thomas' call in this session?

(Probably by ignoring it.)

6. BRINGING IT HOME

Reinforcing Your Point

(5 minutes)

Ask people to read the "Bringing It Home" section of their Participant's Guides later this week. They'll find insights from a counselor on how faith can keep a couple together.

You may want to conclude your meeting with comments like the following.

In our next two sessions we'll be talking more about God's view of our marriages. You'll hear a lot about His purposes for us—which often seem to be at odds with our own.

It will be tempting to nod your head and say, "Yes, I'm all for holiness. Who needs that happiness stuff?" Saying that would sound very spiritual, but might not be very honest. So I encourage you to think this week about those Holiness Meals and Happiness Meals. You may want to ask God to give you an appetite for both.

Close in prayer, making that request on your own behalf—and asking the Lord to give you all a clearer picture of His perspective on your marriages.

IT'S NOT ABOUT YOU

What does the inventor of marriage have to say about it? Why did He bring Adam and Eve together?

Dr. Del Tackett, president of the Focus on the Family Institute and presenter of *The Truth Project*, explains in this DVD segment how God's view of marriage counts the most—and not just because it "works best." Marriage, he says, is a picture of the relationship among the members of the Trinity.

We can't change that—and wouldn't want to, once we begin to grasp its importance.

Session Aim

To help spouses grow closer by working to reflect the oneness of the Trinity, rather than pursuing their own interests only.

Setting the Stage

- Read this session plan and Chapter 2 in the Participant's Guide.
- Provide pencils or pens.
- If you want to use the icebreaker in Step 1, bring two or more common household objects (remote control, can opener, candy bar, etc.) in a bag.
- Cue up the DVD to segment 2, "It's Not About You."

1. GETTING TOGETHER

Optional Icebreaker
(5 minutes)

If your group likes to have fun, or if you're just looking for a way to introduce the topic, try the following.

Bring a paper bag with two or more household items in it—for example, a remote control, a can opener, and a candy bar. Don't let anyone see the items yet.

Form two or more teams. Give them the following instructions.

News flash: Nasty aliens from the planet Jupiter have just landed on the roof. Your job is to save the world! Fortunately, I'm about to give your team a common household object. All you have to do is rescue humanity with it. As soon as you get the object, start acting out what you'd do. You'll have 30 seconds to show us your ingenuity and improvisational skills.

Pick an object from the bag and toss it to someone on the first team. Give the team half a minute to perform its "improv." Applaud the performance and move on to the second team, giving it a different object from the bag. Repeat until you're out of objects and teams.

Then ask: **What is the object you got generally used for?** (Changing TV channels, opening cans, etc.) **Did you know before this meeting that it could be used to save the world?** (Probably not.)

Some pretty common things have uncommon potential—in the right hands. Marriage is that way. We may not save the world anytime soon, but God can use our everyday married lives to accomplish some amazing things—if we let Him.

2. FINDING YOURSELF

Identifying Your Needs
(5-10 minutes)

After having couples turn to the "Finding Yourself" section in the Participant's Guide, invite them to complete the survey found there. Then let volunteers share some of their answers.

1. When you hear someone talk about "God's view of marriage," which of the following best describes your reaction? Why?
    ___ "Who cares?"
    ___ "How interesting that 'God's view' just happens to be yours."
    ___ "I wish I could know what He thinks of my marriage."
    ___ "With all due respect, He's not down here in the trenches."
    ___ "He wants to turn my marriage into a Sunday school class."
    ___ "I want to know His view and let it change the way we live."
    ___ other _____

(Let people express their opinions freely if they're willing to do so.)

2. Which of the following sources are you most likely to turn to for marriage advice? Why?
    ___ friends
    ___ a TV or radio host
    ___ Christian counselor
    ___ non-Christian counselor
    ___ pastor
    ___ the Bible
    ___ another book
    ___ other _____

(After listening to replies, ask which of the sources are most likely to represent God's view.)

3. How might your marriage be different if you lived in the following times and places? Do you think it would better reflect God's view of marriage? Why or why not?
    ___ the Garden of Eden
    ___ Victorian England
    ___ ancient Israel
    ___ the U.S. during World War II
    ___ present-day Afghanistan
    ___ an international space station in the year 2050

(Answers to the first part of the question may vary widely. As for the second part, some participants may assume that marriages of the past better reflected

God's view. You may want to point out that individual marriages could do that at any point in history and at any place.)

4. **Do you believe spouses with a biblical view of marriage are happier than other spouses? Why or why not?** _____
_____

(Opinions will vary. Some surveys indicate that those who attend church most frequently report a higher satisfaction level with their marriages, but church attendance may not reflect having the most biblical view.)

5. **Do you think it matters whether they're happier, as long as they're "right"? Why or why not?** _____
(Answers will differ. Some may feel obeying God leads to happiness in this life, while others may think we have to wait until the next.)

6. **When you got married, did you have a biblical view of marriage? If so, how did you get it? If not, what difference might it have made if you did?** _____
(Responses will vary according to experience. If time allows, ask group members where they'd be most likely to gain a biblical view of marriage today—other than in your group.)

Watching and Discussing the DVD
(20-25 minutes)

After viewing the DVD, use questions like these to help couples think through what they saw and heard.

1. **How would you compare the biblical view of marriage to the perspective offered by the following TV shows? Do you think God's view would make a good premise for a sitcom? Why or why not?**
   • *Trading Spouses*
   • *'Til Death*

- *The Simpsons*
- *Desperate Housewives*

(Most of these shows find comedy or drama in marital conflict. They also tend to follow the characters' efforts to get their needs met by their spouses. In other words, it's all about them—not about accomplishing a higher purpose, much less pleasing God. As for whether God's view would make a good premise for a sitcom, opinions will vary. It might be possible, for example, to mine humor from self-inflicted predicaments that result from ignoring God's view, or from a character's doomed efforts to interest people in God's perspective.)

2. **Dr. Del Tackett calls marriage a sacrificial relationship. If it were legally defined this way, do you think fewer people would get married? Why or why not?**
(Some may think that definition would discourage marriages; others may think people would ignore the definition.)

3. **A self-centered view of marriage leads us to try to get our own way. Which spouse do you think would get his or her own way in each of the following situations? Why? How might the struggle affect each marriage?**
   - **A wife who wants to have children tries to "guilt" her husband (who doesn't want to have children) into changing his mind.**
   - **A husband who wants to host a home Bible study tells his wife (who doesn't want to host one) that the decision is his because he's the spiritual leader of the family.**
   - **A wife who wants to spend $5,000 redecorating the living room tries to pressure her husband (who wants to spend $500) by withholding sex.**
   - **A husband who wants sex more frequently tries to pressure his wife (who wants less) by refusing to talk to her unless absolutely necessary.**
   (These are all cases of manipulation, which might get the desired result in the short run but builds resentment in the long run. Spouses who advance only their own agendas tend to ignore what's best for both partners.)

4. **According to Del, one of the purposes of marriage is to glorify God. How could a husband and wife glorify God in the way they handle the following problems?**

- not being able to have biological children
- living next door to a woman whose dog barks all the time
- taking care of a parent who has Parkinson's disease
- being criticized for having an interracial marriage

(It would be easy to become bitter, self-pitying, or a "martyr" in these situations. Trusting God that He will eventually make things right would not only reduce the couple's stress, but could remind others that God is trustworthy.)

5. **Del says our marriages are meant to reflect the Trinity's awesome unity, intimacy, relationship, and fellowship. Which of those qualities have you seen in another couple's marriage, if only in a small way? What effect has that had on you?**

(Answers will vary. You may want to be ready with an example of your own.)

6. **Del warns against an "I want what I want" attitude. Which of the following have you heard at home? Do they always reflect a "my way" mindset? Why or why not?**
    - **"It's my turn."**
    - **"Don't tell me what to do."**
    - **"You're not my mother."**
    - **"I don't have to put up with this."**
    - **other** _____

(Opinions will differ. Sometimes it really *is* your turn. But the tone of most of these statements indicates an unwillingness to listen to the other person or to discuss the issues further.)

Bible Study
(10 minutes)

For insights from Scripture, have a volunteer read the following passage and discuss the questions that accompany it.

Submit to one another out of reverence for Christ.

Wives, submit to your husbands as to the Lord. For the husband is the head of the wife as Christ is the head of the church, his body, of which he is the Savior. Now as the church submits to Christ, so also wives should submit to their husbands in everything.

Husbands, love your wives, just as Christ loved the church and gave himself up for her to make her holy, cleansing her by the washing with water through the word, and to present her to himself as a radiant church, without stain or wrinkle or any other blemish, but holy and blameless. In this same way, husbands ought to love their wives as their own bodies. He who loves his wife loves himself. After all, no one ever hated his own body, but he feeds and cares for it, just as Christ does the church—for we are members of his body. "For this reason a man will leave his father and mother and be united to his wife, and the two will become one flesh." This is a profound mystery—but I am talking about Christ and the church. However, each one of you also must love his wife as he loves himself, and the wife must respect her husband. (Ephesians 5:21-33)

1. **How is marriage "a profound mystery" to you? How is it not? Do the mysterious parts tend to cause the most trouble, or the more easily explained parts? Can you give an example?**
(Answers will vary; some people may cite the "mysterious" ways of the opposite gender, or wonder how couples stay together for 50 years or more. Yet marital troubles often arise in areas that are more contentious than mysterious—finances, communication, sex, empathy, etc.)

2. **Are there any words in this passage that bother you? If so, can you explain your reaction?**
(Some participants may have misgivings about "submit" and "head," questioning what the roles of men and women should be. Others might wish "holy" weren't there, feeling the standard is too high. Don't try to resolve these issues now; simply acknowledge them.)

3. **What are the differences between the terms in each of the following pairs? Why are the differences important in a marriage?**
   - *submit* and *grovel*
   - *love* and *fondness*
   - *respect* and *fear*

- *holy* and *perfect*
- *head* and *boss*

(Opinions will differ. As needed, you may want to point out that submission is a yielding of one's rights, not a debasing of oneself to placate or impress another, and is for all Christians [verse 21]. Love takes many forms, but is generally more about action [1 Corinthians 13] than it is about emotion or preference. Respect is recognizing a person's authority or value, not being intimidated by him or her [see Luke 12:4-5]; the Bible's instruction to "fear" God is more about giving ultimate respect than about being afraid [see 1 John 4:18]. To be holy is to be set apart for God's use, as many imperfect Bible characters were. Some believe "head" in this passage refers to honor, others to authority, still others to both; "boss" can refer to authority without honor, and can describe one who gives orders without necessarily having earned that right.)

4. **How would you describe the relationship between Christ and the church? How is it like the relationship between spouses? How is it different?**
(Some possibilities: Christ gave His life for the church; He is the Head of it; He wants the best for it; He protects it; He works to improve it. Both relationships are based on love; the authority of Christ over the church, however, is absolute.)

Applying the Principles
(10 minutes)

Have the group turn to the "Making It Work" section in the Participant's Guide. Give people a few minutes to complete the exercise individually, and another few minutes to discuss the results as couples. If time allows, let volunteers share their conclusions with the whole group.

People will differ in their perspectives on the events and what God's view might be. But here are some possible responses.

6:00 A.M.: Alarm doesn't go off. Your spouse inadvertently unplugged it last night, thinking he or she was holding the cord to the cell phone charger.

Your perspective (My spouse is stupid.)

God's perspective (Forgive each other [Luke 6:37].)

7:00 A.M.: Running late for work. No time for breakfast, only for a piece of cold pizza.

Your perspective (My spouse is making my life miserable.)

God's perspective (Don't be in such a hurry [Luke 10:40-42].)

7:59 A.M.: You get a $50 ticket for going 43 miles per hour in a 35-miles-per-hour zone.

Your perspective (I had to do it—and besides, it was my spouse's fault.)

God's perspective (Obey the authorities [Hebrews 13:17].)

9:17 A.M.: In staff meeting, boss names you employee of the month. You'll get to park closer to the building for 30 days, and receive a $50 gift card to your favorite coffee shop.

Your perspective (I'm incredible.)

God's perspective (All good things come from Me [James 1:17].)

11:32 A.M.: Spouse calls, says that if you've gotten over your hissy fit about the alarm not going off, you can meet for lunch. You reply that you've got too much work to do, which isn't quite true.

Your perspective (My spouse doesn't deserve my company.)

God's perspective (Speak the truth in love [Ephesians 4:15].)

12:09 P.M.: Spouse sees you in a restaurant at lunch with two co-workers. Gives you "the look" and leaves, obviously unhappy.

Your perspective (I'm in trouble.)

God's perspective (You're in trouble [Numbers 32:23].)

2:46 P.M.: In a meeting, you make a joke about marriage—comparing it to a minimum-security prison.

Your perspective (I'm clever and funny.)

God's perspective (Marriage should be honored [Hebrews 13:4].)

4:38 P.M.: You leave work early, intending to pick up a small "peacemaking" gift for your spouse. But when you hear a talk radio show about thoughtless spouses, you get mad again and change your mind.

Your perspective (My spouse doesn't deserve a present.)

God's perspective (The anger of man does not accomplish God's purposes [James 1:20].)

5:59 P.M.: Spouse has left a message about being late for dinner. You have another piece of cold pizza.

Your perspective (This is the last straw.)

God's perspective (Love is patient [1 Corinthians 13:4].)

7:00 P.M.: Spouse gets home, but neither of you seems to want to talk. You watch TV alone.

Your perspective (I don't need my spouse.)

God's perspective (The two should become one [Genesis 2:24].)

10:51 P.M.: Still watching TV. Spouse has fallen asleep. You vow to have a conversation about this . . . sometime.

Your perspective (I'll talk about this when I'm good and ready.)

God's perspective (Don't let the sun go down on your anger [Ephesians 4:26].)

If time allows, use questions like the following in discussing people's answers.

Generally speaking, how does our view tend to differ from God's?

(We think of ourselves—our feelings, our goals, our image—and our short-term happiness. God knows what's best for us and for His kingdom in the really long term—eternity.)

If you had a day like the one in this exercise, how could trying to see things from God's perspective help preserve your relationship with your spouse?

(You'd probably attach less importance to every turn of events, be less likely to blame your spouse for everything, be more likely to see your own role in causing problems, and be more forgiving.)

Reinforcing Your Point
(5 minutes)

Remind group members to read the "Bringing It Home" section of their Participant's Guides later this week. They'll find practical insight from a counselor on what a "Christian home" is—and how to have one.

You may want to conclude your meeting with comments like the following.

How can we keep God's perspective in mind this week? Is there something we can carry in our wallets, purses, or pockets to remind us of His view?

(Some suggestions: Post or carry a copy of a Bible verse like 1 Samuel 16:7; carry something that reminds you of time and eternity [an hourglass egg timer or pocket watch]; find an aerial photo of your neighborhood on the Internet [e.g., Google Maps] and use it as a screen saver or bookmark.)

Finding out that your marriage isn't just about you can be a bit of a shock. But it can be freeing, too. Next time we'll talk about the downside of a self-centered marriage, and the upside of serving each other.

If possible, have a volunteer close in prayer—thanking God that our marriages can be a way not only to enjoy His invention of intimacy, but also to glorify Him.

TRUTH AND CONSEQUENCES

What happens when our take on marriage doesn't match God's perspective? Instead of asking how we can serve our spouses, we concentrate on getting our needs met. Sometimes those aren't needs at all—just wants.

Dr. Del Tackett returns in this DVD segment, challenging couples to live out the implications of God's view. How can we love and respect each other more? How can we become one? How can we better reflect our Creator's character?

The truth about marriage has consequences, and couples who live accordingly will be glad they did.

Session Aim

To help husbands and wives practice serving God and each other instead of being self-serving.

Setting the Stage

- Read this session plan and Chapter 3 in the Participant's Guide.
- Provide pencils or pens.
- If you want to use the "Harmony" icebreaker in Step 1, bring a prize for the best impromptu orchestra.
- Cue up the DVD to segment 3, "Truth and Consequences."

Optional Icebreaker
(5 minutes)

For groups that need a warm-up, or who just like to have fun, here's an opener to try.

Form two teams. Your challenge: **We're going to have a harmony contest. Find anything you can to make music, and try to make it all fit together. The most harmonious instant orchestra wins.**

Give people one minute to find their "instruments" (cell phone ringtones, oatmeal boxes and spoons, radios, guitars, voices, whistles, squeeze toys, etc.). Then give them another minute to practice before performing for the whole group.

After the concert, applaud the bands and award your prize. Discuss the contest, using questions like these:

On a scale of 1 to 10 (10 being most difficult), how hard was it to be harmonious with your collection of instruments? Why?

(Answers will vary, but it's likely to have been pretty tough to get beautiful music from these motley orchestras.)

How do you think this harmony compares with the harmony we'll experience in heaven?

(Probably not favorably. Besides the harmony generated by worshipers and angelic choirs, the relational harmony of the Father, Son, and Holy Spirit will be perfect.)

Believe it or not, our marriages were designed to echo the harmony of heaven. We may not have a lot to work with, but at least we have more than a minute to put it together. Let's find out how it's supposed to go—and what happens when it doesn't.

Identifying Your Needs
(5-10 minutes)

Draw the group's attention to the "Finding Yourself" section in the Participant's Guide.

Here are some questions about the viewpoints you might be bringing to this meeting. Take a couple of minutes to answer them; then let's discuss them as a group.

1. Which of the following is closest to your reaction when you hear that marriage is supposed to last a lifetime?

    ___ "Not anymore."

    ___ "That's absolutely right."

    ___ "Then I've already blown it."

    ___ "Impossible."

    ___ "Unfortunately, yes."

    ___ other _____

    (Opinions will vary; avoid trying to correct any questionable reactions at this point.)

2. Which of the following do you think you understand as well as you need to? Which are you uncertain about?

    ___ God's view of divorce

    ___ why the Bible prohibits adultery

    ___ why God invented marriage

    ___ the biblical view of same-sex "marriage"

    ___ your spouse's opinions on these subjects

    (Replies will differ; you may want to note issues participants seem especially interested in or confused about, in order to address them at another time.)

3. Which of the following do you think are good reasons to stay married? How would you rank them in order from least important to most? Why?

    ___ for the sake of the children

    ___ to avoid the embarrassment of divorce

    ___ because God said so

    ___ because your parents stayed married

    ___ due to peer or family pressure

    ___ for financial stability

    (Rankings will vary, though many people may put "because God said so" at the top of the list because it's the "right" answer. Ask them why they'd put it there.)

4. **Have you ever done something you knew was wrong? If so, why did you do it anyway?** _____

_____

(Participants needn't provide details; the point is to establish that people often make the wrong choices when they know what the right ones are.)

5. **When it comes to marriage, what kinds of things do some spouses do that they probably know are wrong? Why?** _____

(Some possibilities: infidelity, hiding financial information from each other, being abusive, holding a grudge.)

6. **How much would someone have to pay you to take an "unbiblical" approach to marriage? Why?**

____ **$1,000,000,000**

____ **$1,000,000**

____ **$100,000**

____ **$10,000**

____ **no amount of money would be enough**

____ **no money would be necessary**

____ **other** _____

(Answers may vary; some group members may want to know what moral issue might be at stake before attaching a dollar value. The important thing is to get people thinking about how committed they are to the Bible's authority in their married lives.)

3. CATCHING THE VISION

Watching and Discussing the DVD
(20-25 minutes)

After viewing the DVD, use questions like these to help couples think through what they saw and heard.

1. **How would you describe the tone of Dr. Del Tackett's presentation on the DVD? Do you think it's appropriate for the subject? Why or why not?**

- exciting
- sorrowful
- awed
- condemning
- other _____

(Answers will vary, though he seems mostly awed about the majesty of God's plan for marriage and sorrowful about those who ignore it.)

2. **What happens when people defy God's laws or instructions in the following areas? How soon would you expect the consequences to be obvious?**
   - **gravity**
   - **adultery**
   - **being good stewards of creation**
   - **honoring parents**
   - **keeping a vow to stay married**

(Defying gravity without a parachute could be fatal, as would be obvious immediately. The emotional fallout of adultery might be seen quickly, though the spiritual results might not be clear until the next life. Poor stewardship of creation has consequences over time—disease, starvation, loss of natural beauty and animal species. Dishonoring parents leads to broken relationships and possibly a shorter life [Exodus 20:12]. Breaking marriage vows may seem to have no consequences in the short run but often hurts spouses and children for the rest of their lives.)

3. **Del is "the product of divorced parents." In your opinion, does that affect his credibility when talking about the results of ignoring God's view of marriage? If so, how?**
   (Some may have reservations about anyone from a "broken home," but most probably will feel that Del has firsthand knowledge of the pain of divorce.)

4. **How would you respond to someone who made the following statements? What kind of reply would you expect to get?**
   - **"God has bigger things to worry about than how I treat my spouse."**
   - **"I can't believe God would expect me to stay in an unhappy marriage."**

- "My wedding vows don't count; I was too young when I made them."
- "Fantasies aren't real; they don't affect my marriage."

(Responses will vary. The statements make some false assumptions—that God can deal with only one issue at a time, that our "happiness" is His top priority, that promises are temporary, and individuals are the best judges of whether their actions affect others. Since these are all rationalizations, we could expect more excuses.)

5. **On a scale of 1 to 10 (10 highest), how would you rate the truthfulness of the following ideas? How would you rate their importance?**
    - **We don't need Satan to wreck our marriages; we're quite capable of doing it on our own.**
    - **There can be nothing more glorious on earth than following God's design.**
    - **There's no place for violence, verbal abuse, or rudeness in marriage.**

(Group members may rate the ideas highly; if so, challenge them to explain why they're important.)

6. **According to Malachi 2:16, God hates divorce. How might each of the following people react to hearing this? How might they react to Del's explanation that this isn't just a pragmatic statement about the pain divorce brings, but grief over tearing apart the intimacy that reflects God's nature?**
    - **a divorce lawyer**
    - **a recently divorced person**
    - **a child whose parents divorced 20 years ago**
    - **a person considering divorce**

(Answers may vary widely. Some might assume that a divorce lawyer, a recently divorced person, and a person considering divorce would be "in favor" of the practice, but they might also be especially aware of the hurt it brings. A child of divorce probably would know and relive that pain, though in cases of abuse might see the divorce as an escape. As for people's reaction to the biblical view, that would depend on whether they see Scripture as God's Word or just another book.)

7. **After watching the DVD, which of these people do you feel most like? Why?**
     - **Del, when he confronted the couple having the adulterous affair**
     - **the young woman who didn't think she could trust a man after her father left her mother**
     - **the unfaithful spouses who seemed unaffected by God's Word**

   (Feelings and explanations will vary.)

8. **Del observes that God wants us to experience in marriage something of the wonder and beauty found in the relationship among the Persons of the Trinity—which leads to life, peace, and happiness. Which of the following steps would you take first to start experiencing that?**
     - **learning more about God's nature by reading the Bible**
     - **talking with your spouse about your relationship**
     - **asking God to help you understand what He wants your marriage to be**
     - **other** _____

   (There is no "right" answer here. Encourage couples to choose a "next step" that's small enough to actually take this week.)

Bible Study
(10 minutes)

If your group has been organized with Bible study in mind, have volunteers read these passages and discuss the questions that follow them.

> *The wrath of God is being revealed from heaven against all the godlessness and wickedness of men who suppress the truth by their wickedness, since what may be known about God is plain to them, because God has made it plain to them. For since the creation of the world God's invisible qualities—his eternal power and divine nature—have been clearly seen, being understood from what has been made, so that men are without excuse. . . .*

Therefore God gave them over in the sinful desires of their hearts to sexual impurity for the degrading of their bodies with one another. They exchanged the truth of God for a lie, and worshiped and served created things rather than the Creator—who is forever praised. Amen. (Romans 1:18-20, 24-25)

1. **What is the "truth of God" when it comes to marriage?**
   (Some possible answers: That it was meant to be a lifelong relationship; that it was designed for one man and one woman; that it involves an exclusive sexual relationship; that it has a higher purpose than just personal fulfillment; that it's based on respect and love.)

2. **What "lie" have some spouses exchanged it for?**
   (That marriage is temporary; that it's not gender-specific; that it's not realistic to expect sexual fidelity; that it's about getting your needs met; that it's based on power struggles, hormones, or fleeting feelings.)

3. **Do you think the apostle Paul would be shocked by some current attitudes toward marriage, or would they remind him of his own culture? Why?**
   (Opinions will differ; given the situations he wrote about in some of his letters, however, our society might remind him of his own.)

   Why be captivated, my son, by an adulteress? Why embrace the bosom of another man's wife?
   For a man's ways are in full view of the LORD, and he examines all his paths. The evil deeds of a wicked man ensnare him; the cords of his sin hold him fast. He will die for lack of discipline, led astray by his own great folly. (Proverbs 5:20-23)

4. **What answers might an unfaithful spouse give to the questions in this passage? What answers are implied in many TV shows, movies, and popular songs?**
   (An unfaithful spouse who regretted his or her actions might ask the same questions. One seeking to justify his or her actions might blame a spouse who was "boring," "cold," or "cheating on me." Popular culture often does the same, or excuses infidelity as the result of unstoppable emotions or all-powerful hormones.)

5. **If everything we do is "in full view of the LORD," why do so many people—even some Christians—seem to think He won't see what they do? If God's presence were observable, do you think there would be fewer extramarital affairs? Why or why not?**

   (Responses will vary. Even some people who claim to believe God is watching assume He'll make an exception in their case, or that He's so forgiving that He couldn't possibly punish them for disobeying. Others are too focused on their own unmet emotional needs or sexual desires to care what God might think. If His presence could be observed, overt affairs might be less frequent—but given human nature, adulterous thoughts might be as common as ever.)

6. **Based on what you see around you, when does sexual sin usually take its toll? Why might some believe they can get away with "evil deeds"?**

   (People are often "ensnared" quickly, addicted to pornography or seemingly unable to break off an affair. Other effects, such as sexually transmitted diseases or the inability to form an intimate relationship, might be clear later. In some cases the results aren't seen in this life, which may explain why many people count on evading the consequences.)

Applying the Principles
(10 minutes)

Ask people to find the "Making It Work" section of the Participant's Guide. Give them several minutes to complete the exercise, working as couples. Then, if time allows, let volunteers tell the rest of the group which favors were most favored.

Why is it important to know whether your spouse values one favor over another?

(If you really want to serve your spouse, you'll concentrate on the things he or she most needs and wants; if you don't understand what your spouse values, you may be disappointed when he or she doesn't seem to appreciate what you've done.)

Why might one spouse see an action as a great sacrifice, while the other barely notices it?

(What's easy for one person may be difficult for another; one spouse might think a task is meant for the opposite sex, based on his or her upbringing; a task can seem harder if you're resentful about it; one spouse may feel entitled and take the other's work for granted.)

Did you pick two favors to do for your spouse this week? If so, how did you choose them?

(Answers will vary. Ideally, choices would be based on the other person's needs and preferences.)

Reinforcing Your Point
(5 minutes)

Ask group members to read the "Bringing It Home" section of their Participant's Guides later this week. This time they'll find a counselor's advice on what to do when self-serving attitudes have damaged a relationship.

Being a servant to your spouse isn't exactly a popular idea, especially these days. Maybe that's why, if you look up quotations about marriage, you'll find plenty like these:

> **Women have their faults. Men have only two:**
> **Everything they say. Everything they do.**
>
> *—Anonymous*

> **The fastest way to a man's heart is through his chest.**
>
> *—Roseanne Arnold*

> **On quiet nights, when I am alone, I like to run our wedding video backwards, just to watch myself walk out of the church a free man.**
>
> *—George Coote*

> **If you think women are the weaker sex, try pulling the blankets back to your side.**
>
> *—Stuart Turner*

A man with pierced ears is better prepared for marriage. He has experienced pain and bought jewelry.

—*Rita Rudner*

If we laugh at lines like that, maybe it's because we know that serving each other isn't always easy. But it makes a marriage work. More importantly, it pleases the One who invented marriage in the first place.

You might want to have a volunteer conclude the session by praying for couples who'll be working on servanthood this week.

ACHIEVING SPIRITUAL INTIMACY

Plenty of Christians would say that faith should bring couples closer. But does it? Not if the only "faith-based" thing you do is sitting next to each other in church.

In this DVD segment, a battery of experts tell how to apply the principle of marital oneness to the spiritual side of your relationship. Gary Thomas urges husbands to pray for their wives; Stormie Omartian explains the benefits of praying and praising as a couple; Dr. Gary and Barb Rosberg deliver tips on praying together.

Finally, Drs. Les and Leslie Parrott tell how opening their home and taking on service projects has brought them closer—and can do the same for you.

Session Aim
To help spouses plan ways to grow closer through praying, praising, and serving God as a team.

Setting the Stage
- Read this session plan and Chapter 4 in the Participant's Guide.
- Provide pencils or pens.
- To use the optional "Mission Undoable" icebreaker in Step 1, photocopy the coded instructions (one copy for every two people) or write them on white board, chalkboard, or large newsprint.
- Cue up the DVD to segment 4, "Achieving Spiritual Intimacy."

1. GETTING TOGETHER

Optional Icebreaker
(5 minutes)

This session is about accomplishing the "mission" of marriage. So here's a chance for your group to tackle a mission that's more or less impossible.

Before the session, photocopy the following assignment (one copy for every two people). Or, if your group is large, write the coded mission on a white board or other display surface.

TOP SECRET

Your mission, whether or not you decide to accept it:

HFU UIF HSPVQ
MFBEFS UP MFBWF
UIF SPPN

Form random pairs. Give each pair a copy of the "mission" (unless you've written it so that the whole group can see it). Then give the following instructions.

You're on a top-secret mission. It's in code, of course. But to make it easier, I'm going to impose two simple rules.

First, you have only one minute to accomplish your mission. Second, you can't get within 10 feet of your partner. If you don't accomplish your mission, your team will self-destruct in 60 seconds.

Teams probably will complain that the mission is impossible. Some may try to decipher the code. By the time the minute is up, most participants will be ready for your self-destruction, if not their own.

Then reveal the mission: GET THE GROUP LEADER TO LEAVE THE ROOM. In the unlikely event that someone figured it out, congratulate the decoder. (The code is simple; each letter stands for the one that comes before it in the alphabet.)

Then ask: **Why was this a tough assignment?**

(We couldn't understand the mission, couldn't get close enough to work together, and didn't have enough time.)

We've been talking about God's purpose for our marriages. What are some things that stand in the way of accomplishing that mission?

(We have our own goals; we aren't clear on what He wants for us; we're afraid we'll be miserable if we aren't concentrating on our own happiness; we can't get close enough to work together.)

God has some spiritual goals for our marriages. Working toward those goals as a couple can bring us closer together—and help our marriages endure. There are obstacles on the way to accomplishing that mission, but in this session we'll talk about how to overcome them.

2. FINDING YOURSELF

Identifying Your Needs
(5-10 minutes)

Here are some questions to ask yourself.

1. **What's your response when you hear that spouses should pray together?**
   ___ **"That's for super-spiritual people."**
   ___ **"We tried that, but it didn't work for us."**
   ___ **"It would feel forced and fake."**
   ___ **"I know we should, but we never get around to it."**
   ___ **"We do, and I'm glad."**
   ___ **other** _____

   (Answers will vary, but probably will reflect the awkwardness or guilt many people feel about not praying as a couple.)

2. **If you and your spouse got involved in a service project, what would you want it to be? Why?**
    ___ serving food in a soup kitchen
    ___ visiting people in a nursing home
    ___ protesting an injustice
    ___ going on a mission trip to another country
    ___ short and sweet
    ___ other _____

    (Listen to replies; if time allows, let one or two couples describe a service project they undertook as a team.)

3. **Have you ever known a husband and wife who made ministry a priority in their marriage? If so, what were they like?**
    ___ boring
    ___ admirable but out of our league
    ___ surprisingly normal
    ___ fun
    ___ obnoxious and hypocritical
    ___ other _____

    (Answers may vary. You might ask whether the couple's personality influenced people to make ministry a priority, too.)

4. **What do you think is your spouse's most urgent prayer request right now? If you can't answer this question, how do you feel about that?**

    _____

    _____

    (People may want to answer this question to their spouses only.)

5. **On a scale of 1 to 10 (10 highest), how well do you and your spouse work as a team? How do you know?** _____
    (This may be another couples-only question.)

6. **Do you think couples need a "mission statement"? Why or why not?**

    _____

    (Opinions may differ. If any group members have come up with mission statements of their own, invite them to share the statements.)

Watching and Discussing the DVD
(20-25 minutes)

After viewing the DVD, use questions like these to help couples think through
what they saw and heard.

1. **Which kind of intimacy do you think is most important to the long-term
   success of a marriage: emotional, physical, or spiritual? Why? If you could
   have only one of them, which would you choose? Why? In an average
   week, about how much time do you devote to building each?**
   (Replies will vary; some may point out that spiritual intimacy is the deepest,
   so it stands to reason that it would have the greatest effect. That may be true,
   but encourage those who answer this way to give a concrete example.)

2. **According to Gary Thomas, praying for your spouse creates empathy—
   helping you see the day through his or her eyes. If you prayed for your
   spouse on a typical weekday at the following times, what specifically
   would you pray about? How would you want your spouse to pray for you
   at those times?**
   - **8:00 A.M.**
   - **noon**
   - **5:15 P.M.**
   - **10:00 P.M.**
   (Answers, like schedules, will differ. To save time, have people discuss this with
   their spouses rather than with the whole group.)

3. **Gary notes that many men seem afraid to pray with their wives. What
   might be scaring them? Do you think most wives feel the same way about
   praying with their husbands? Why or why not?**
   (Some men may fear their wives will use the opportunity to preach at
   them, or may fear embarrassing themselves by saying the "wrong" thing or
   getting emotional. Some may suggest that praying aloud comes more natu-
   rally to women because they tend to be more verbal; ask wives how they feel
   about it.)

4. **Stormie Omartian says that praying and worshiping as a couple are the most powerful things you can do together. If you're already doing those things, which of the following obstacles did you overcome to get started? If not, which would be worth overcoming to give it a try? Which obstacle would you tackle first? Why?**
   - lack of time
   - feeling embarrassed to pray or worship outside of a church meeting
   - not wanting to reveal deep emotions or personal thoughts
   - thinking it's not worth the effort
   - assuming it's only for super-spiritual people
   - not knowing how
   - other _____

   (If this is too personal for your group members to discuss with the group, have them talk about it as couples.)

5. **Stormie observes that when you pray and praise together, strife is lifted from you. Dr. Gary and Barb Rosberg put it another way: It's hard to be mad at your mate when you pray together. Which of the following might account for that?**
   - When you pray together, it forces you to agree.
   - Prayer and worship remind you that God is watching and listening.
   - You'd feel guilty about fighting after you pray.
   - Prayer and praise remind you that God is in charge, leading you to be humble.
   - Prayer and praise help you focus on your real priorities and common ground.
   - other _____

   (Answers will vary. As needed, point out that prayer doesn't *force* you to agree—though it may ease the way to agreement by reminding you of God's perspective.)

6. **The Rosbergs note that prayer doesn't change the nature of God—it changes us. How would you like prayer to change you during the next six months?**
   - I'd like to feel closer to my spouse.

- **I'd like to feel closer to God.**
- **I'd like to feel my spouse and I are going in the right direction together.**
- **other** _____

(Replies will differ; some might find it hard to answer because they've concentrated on trying to change their spouses, not themselves.)

7. **The Rosbergs warn against using prayer with your spouse as a chance to preach at him or her. Which of the following prayers would you put in that category? Why?**
   - **"Lord, help my husband to be the man You want him to be."**
   - **"Thank You that You have raised up counselors to whom we should go when we are depressed."**
   - **"May we remember that Your Word tells us that a wife is to submit to her husband."**
   - **"We know that You will make it clear whether we should vacation in Hawaii or serve You building houses in Guatemala."**

(Any of these could be manipulative, depending on the mindset of the person praying and the discussions the spouses have had before about these subjects.)

8. **Drs. Les and Leslie Parrott say that practicing hospitality or otherwise serving together unites spouses, stimulates conversation between them, builds intimacy, and helps them fulfill their purpose. Which of these benefits appeals to you most? How might your hospitality or service benefit the recipients?**
   (Answers will vary.)

9. **Which of the following suggestions from this session are you willing to try this week?**
   - **Take turns praying a sentence at a time.**
   - **Invite other couples into your home.**
   - **Sponsor a needy child together.**
   - **Do a "Shared Service in Secret" project.**
   - **Become a marriage mentor to another couple.**
   - **Ask another couple to mentor you.**

(To generate as much discussion as time allows, have participants talk about this as couples rather than with the whole group. Encourage them to continue the discussion this week.)

4. DIGGING DEEPER

Bible Study
(10 minutes)

For insights from Scripture, have volunteers read the following passages and discuss the questions that accompany them.

> *Now a man named Ananias, together with his wife Sapphira, also sold a piece of property. With his wife's full knowledge he kept back part of the money for himself, but brought the rest and put it at the apostles' feet.*
>
> *Then Peter said, "Ananias, how is it that Satan has so filled your heart that you have lied to the Holy Spirit and have kept for yourself some of the money you received for the land? Didn't it belong to you before it was sold? And after it was sold, wasn't the money at your disposal? What made you think of doing such a thing? You have not lied to men but to God."*
>
> *When Ananias heard this, he fell down and died. And great fear seized all who heard what had happened. Then the young men came forward, wrapped up his body, and carried him out and buried him.*
>
> *About three hours later his wife came in, not knowing what had happened. Peter asked her, "Tell me, is this the price you and Ananias got for the land?"*
>
> *"Yes," she said, "that is the price."*
>
> *Peter said to her, "How could you agree to test the Spirit of the Lord? Look! The feet of the men who buried your husband are at the door, and they will carry you out also."*
>
> *At that moment she fell down at his feet and died. Then the young men came in and, finding her dead, carried her out and buried her beside her husband. Great fear seized the whole church and all who heard about these events. (Acts 5:1-11)*

1. **In what way did Ananias and Sapphira "live out their purpose together"? Why wasn't that an admirable thing?**

(The two of them worked together to keep as much money as possible while looking as "spiritual" as possible. They did work as a team, but in pursuit of the wrong mission.)

2. **What role do you think these spouses allowed God to have in their marriage? Where do you think they went wrong?**
(Perhaps they wanted the acceptance of other believers, but saw God as too distant to care what they were doing. They valued appearance, not reality.)

3. **How do some couples try to "outvote" God and take their own direction in the following areas? What might be the consequences?**
   - **making decisions about having children**
   - **giving to the church**
   - **choosing movies to watch**
   - **buying cars**
   - **inviting others into their home**

(Rather than taking time to debate the issues involved in these decisions, keep the discussion focused on the fact that, like Ananias and Sapphira, many of us want to substitute our agendas for God's. The consequences may not be as severe as those suffered by the couple in Acts, but ignoring or trying to deceive God can become a lifelong pattern that puts distance between us and Him.)

When Joseph and Mary had done everything required by the Law of the Lord, they returned to Galilee to their own town of Nazareth. And the child grew and became strong; he was filled with wisdom, and the grace of God was upon him.

Every year his parents went to Jerusalem for the Feast of the Passover. When he was twelve years old, they went up to the Feast, according to the custom. After the Feast was over, while his parents were returning home, the boy Jesus stayed behind in Jerusalem, but they were unaware of it. Thinking he was in their company, they traveled on for a day. Then they began looking for him among their relatives and friends. When they did not find him, they went back to Jerusalem to look for him. After three days they found him in the temple courts, sitting among the teachers, listening to them and asking them questions. Everyone who heard him was amazed at his understanding and his answers. When his parents saw him, they were astonished. His mother said to him, "Son, why have you treated us like this? Your father and I have been anxiously searching for you."

"Why were you searching for me?" he asked. "Didn't you know I had to be in my Father's house?" But they did not understand what he was saying to them.

Then he went down to Nazareth with them and was obedient to them. But his mother treasured all these things in her heart. And Jesus grew in wisdom and stature, and in favor with God and men. (Luke 2:39-52)

4. **What purpose did Mary and Joseph live out together in this passage? What did it cost them to do that?**

   (They were trying to raise Jesus in a God-honoring way; in this incident that meant enduring the fear and inconvenience of letting Jesus accomplish the mission His Father had given Him.)

5. **What made Mary and Joseph different from Ananias and Sapphira?**

   (They were pursuing God's purposes instead of their own.)

6. **Did Mary and Joseph completely understand God's view of their purpose? If not, how did they manage to live it out anyway?**

   (It's doubtful that they fully understood the "big story" while they were living it. But they followed the instructions God had specifically given them, as well as the general directions already available in His Word.)

7. **What was the result of this couple's teamwork?**

   (Jesus matured as He was supposed to, and eventually accomplished everything He'd been assigned to do—including making eternal life available to everyone who believes in Him.)

Applying the Principles
(10 minutes)

After turning to the "Making It Work" section in the Participant's Guide, give couples several minutes to complete the service project planning activity. Let volunteers share their ideas with the group, even if they aren't finished or aren't sure whether or when they'll be able to turn their plans into reality.

Then ask: **Who do you think will benefit more from your project—the givers or the receivers? Why?**

How could our group help with your project? Are there any opportunities to combine your project with that of another couple? Would that keep you from growing closer as spouses? Why or why not?

(Answers will vary. Some couples might welcome the involvement of others, while some might prefer to do "their" project alone.)

Reinforcing Your Point
(5 minutes)

Remind people that the "Bringing It Home" section of their Participant's Guides contains good advice they can read during the week. This week's insight comes from a counselor who explains how couples can start doing something that might seem awkward at first—praying together.

Here are comments you might use in wrapping up your meeting.

This session was full of ideas for getting closer spiritually. One was to take turns praying a sentence at a time with your spouse. Let's close our meeting by trying that. Get together as couples, and for the next minute or so take turns praying just a sentence at a time. Pray about anything that's on your mind.

If you think your group isn't ready for this, conclude by praying yourself. Ask God to help spouses grow closer to each other by growing closer to Him.

MARRIAGE MYTHS AND EXPECTATIONS

When you got married, what did you expect?

In this DVD segment, host Dr. Greg Smalley, along with marriage and family therapist Mitch Temple, talks about the disappointment and conflict that can arise from misconceptions of wedded bliss. Mitch reveals some top myths that can wreck marriages.

And both of these experts explain how aligning our expectations and beliefs with reality can keep us together.

Session Aim

To help spouses drop unrealistic expectations that can erode their marriages, and to replace those myths with reality-based beliefs.

Setting the Stage

- Read this session plan and Chapter 5 in the Participant's Guide.
- Provide pencils or pens.
- If you want to use the icebreaker in Step 1, bring a box of assorted chocolates (enough for each person to have one).
- Cue up the DVD to segment 5, "Marriage Myths and Expectations."

Optional Icebreaker
(5 minutes)

Here's a painless (and tasty) way to begin your meeting, not to mention introducing the topic of expectations.

Bring a box of assorted chocolates, enough that each person can have a piece. If you can find the kind with a chart that names the type of candy found in each spot in the box, so much the better. Before the meeting, move the chocolates around in the box so that they don't match the chart.

As people arrive, offer each one a chocolate. Ask participants not to eat the candy yet.

When everyone has a chocolate, ask people to guess what kind of candy they have. Let them consult the chart if you have one. Then have them eat the candy.

Ask: **Did you get what you expected? Was anybody disappointed? Pleasantly surprised?**

(Most people might be satisfied with what they got—but if the shape of a candy or its location on a chart misled them, they'll at least be surprised.)

In the movie *Forrest Gump*, Forrest's mother says, "Life's a box of chocolates, Forrest. You never know what you're gonna get." That's often true in marriage, too. Our guesses and expectations can be miles from reality—especially if we believe some dangerous marriage myths. That's what this session is about.

Identifying Your Needs
(5-10 minutes)

After having people turn to the "Finding Yourself" section in the participant's guide, invite them to work their way through the questionnaire as couples. If time allows, you can then discuss questions 1, 4, 5, and 6 as a group.

1. When you were growing up, which of the following TV shows had the most influence on your mental picture of marriage? What kind of influence did they have?

    ___ *Married with Children*

    ___ *Mad About You*

    ___ *The Cosby Show*

    ___ *Everybody Loves Raymond*

    ___ *Family Guy*

    ___ *According to Jim*

    ___ *The Brady Bunch*

    ___ other _____

(Answers will vary. Some people may have been strongly influenced by what they saw on TV, though most probably were shaped more decisively by their parents' example.)

2. Which of the following assumptions did you grow up with? Why? How do they compare with your spouse's expectations?

    ___ The husband keeps the car running and the house repaired.

    ___ The wife does most of the cooking.

    ___ Housekeeping chores should be shared about equally.

    ___ The husband keeps track of the money.

    ___ The wife should earn less than the husband.

    ___ The wife should stay home when the children are young.

(Remind couples that they're only to compare expectations, not debate which ones are "better.")

3. Which of the following questions did you and your spouse-to-be discuss before marriage? Which did you not discuss but wish you had?

    ___ "Do you want to have children?"

    ___ "What church do you want to go to?"

    ___ "Which *Star Trek* captain do you like best?"

    ___ "How much should we save, spend, and give?"

    ___ "Are you a convicted felon?"

    ___ "How often do you want to visit your parents?"

(Encourage couples to keep discussing this question during the week.)

4. **Based on your experience, what do you think are the three biggest myths about marriage?** _____

_____

(Some participants may be reluctant to answer if they think "based on your experience" refers to their own marriages. Explain that they're welcome to answer on the basis of observing other couples, too.)

5. **What surprised you most about married life?** _____

_____

(If group members hesitate to reply because they don't want to reveal disappointment with a mate, it may help to be ready with an example from your own marriage that your spouse wouldn't object to.)

6. **Do you think premarital counseling should be required by law? Why or why not?** _____

_____

(Opinions will differ. Premarital counseling can help couples examine their expectations, which is important; making it mandatory is debatable.)

Watching and Discussing the DVD
(20-25 minutes)

Once you've viewed the DVD, use questions like these to spur discussion.

1. **Which of the following expectations did you bring to your marriage, only to find they didn't match reality?**
   - **We'll go out as often as we did before we got married.**
   - **She (or he) will always look this way.**
   - **Our marriage will be like my parents'.**
   - **All we need is love.**
   - **other** _____

(Participants' willingness to reply may depend on whether their answers imply dissatisfaction with their spouse. If possible, be ready with an example of your own.)

2. **From which of the following did you get most of your assumptions about marriage? If you have children, where do you think they'll get theirs?**
   - **TV and movies**
   - **your parents' teaching**
   - **your parents' example**
   - **the Bible**
   - **other** _____

   (Answers will differ; you may want to point out, though, that the strongest influence on children usually is their parents.)

3. **Mitch Temple talks about the marriage myth that says, "As long as we're happy, that's the most important thing." Mitch notes that commitment is more important to successful marriages. What role do you think happiness plays in marriage? Where does it come from?**
   (Replies will vary. Some may think happiness flows from commitment.)

4. **Another marriage myth: "I made a mistake; I didn't marry my soul mate." How do you think the idea that there's only one "right" person for everyone got started? Is it less romantic to believe that a soul mate is something you become, not someone you find? Is it less spiritual? Why or why not?**
   (Ancient Greek philosopher Plato thought that humans originally had four legs, four arms, and one head with two faces—only to be split in half by Zeus. As a result, they had to look for their other halves, their soul mates. It may be a romantic notion, but it's not spiritual in the biblical sense.)

5. **Still another marriage myth: "I can change my spouse." What do you think would be Mitch's advice to Spouse A in each of the following situations?**
   - **Spouse A has always hated Spouse B's loud nose-blowing.**
   - **Spouse A wishes Spouse B would learn to balance a checkbook.**

- **Spouse A fears riding in the car with Spouse B, who is a careless driver.**
- **Spouse A rarely sees Spouse B, who spends six hours a day playing online video games.**

(Mitch says that trying to change your spouse's personality to meet your expectations is unfair. It's also highly unlikely that you'll be able to do it. The only person you can change is yourself. When the issue is a specific behavior, however, such as noisy nose-blowing or playing video games for six hours a day, a healthy relationship allows for negotiation. Spouse A may need to change his or her own expectations about what nose-blowing is "supposed" to sound like. On the other hand, six hours a day of video games is likely to prevent all kinds of intimacy, causing long-term damage to the relationship, and needs to be resolved.)

6. **How could each of the following myths "poison" a marriage? What truth would be an antidote to each statement?**
   - **"It doesn't matter how we treat each other if we're married."**
   - **"A crisis means our marriage is over."**

(The first myth leads at best to taking each other for granted, and at worst to abuse. The second can cause spouses to avoid crisis by sweeping conflict under the rug, or seeing divorce as the only "solution" when problems arise. Possible antidotes: "Married people are to treat each other with love and respect"; "Crisis can be a bridge to a stronger marriage.")

7. **One more marriage myth: "My attitude has nothing to do with it." How would you describe this attitude in three words? How would you describe in three words the attitudes reflected in each of the other myths? Which myth do you most need to question or reject this week?**

(Examples: "My attitude has nothing to do with it" might be expressed as "I'm always right" or "Feelings don't matter." "I can change my spouse" could be boiled down to "You're the problem" or "I control others." People's assessments of which myths they need to question or reject will vary. Avoid pressing for explanations of this answer, since they might be too personal to share.)

Note: For more information on these and other marriage myths, see *The Marriage Turnaround* by Mitch Temple (Moody Publishers, 2009).

4. DIGGING DEEPER

Bible Study
(10 minutes)

Is Scripture study one of your group's primary goals? If so, have volunteers read some or all of the following passages and talk about the questions that follow them.

> *Many a man claims to have unfailing love, but a faithful man who can find?* (Proverbs 20:6)

1. **Why do so many spouses promise that their love will never fail, only to "fall out of love"? How do your beliefs about love affect your ability to remain faithful?**
   (If you believe love is simply a feeling, or that it just "happens" to you, it's harder to stay committed.)

> *It is a trap for a man to dedicate something rashly and only later to consider his vows. (Proverbs 20:25)*

2. **What percentage of couples do you think enter marriage "rashly" and later regret it? How could changing their expectations help to solve this problem?**
   (Guesses will vary; many people have moments when they regret getting married, whether they did so rashly or not. A clear-eyed view of marriage's ups and downs might help them weather the challenges.)

> *Do not boast about tomorrow, for you do not know what a day may bring forth. (Proverbs 27:1)*

3. **What does this proverb have to say to a husband or wife who thinks, *I can change my spouse*?**
   (Thinking you can change your spouse may be more naïve than arrogant, but it claims a power none of us has. And since none of us can predict the future, it's unwise to base yours on speculation.)

He who works his land will have abundant food, but the one who chases fantasies will have his fill of poverty. (Proverbs 28:19)

4. **Is a spouse with unrealistic expectations "chasing fantasies"? Why or why not?**
(Answers may vary. But unrealistic expectations—for instance, believing that your spouse will always cook you breakfast or give you the perfect birthday gift—belong in the realm of fantasy.)

Charm is deceptive, and beauty is fleeting; but a woman who fears the LORD is to be praised. (Proverbs 31:30)

5. **If all husbands understood this verse when they got married, how might the infidelity rate be affected? How does it apply to wives as well?**
(If both husbands and wives stopped expecting their spouses to remain as charming and physically attractive as they seemed during courtship, they might be less disillusioned later and less likely to stray. They might also place a higher value on qualities that last, such as "fearing the Lord.")

When times are good, be happy; but when times are bad, consider: God has made the one as well as the other. Therefore, a man cannot discover anything about his future. (Ecclesiastes 7:14)

6. **When you got married, did you think there were more good times ahead than bad ones? Did things turn out as you expected? How could this verse help a couple who's having a difficult year?**
(It's natural, and probably healthy, for newlyweds to be optimistic. But life includes suffering as well as celebration, and we can't know what the proportions will be. Knowing that God is in control at both times could help a couple who mistakenly expected things to go smoothly.)

May your fountain be blessed, and may you rejoice in the wife of your youth. (Proverbs 5:18)

7. When was the last time you "rejoiced in the [spouse] of your youth" by re-
calling what attracted you when you first met? What are three of his or her
qualities that led you to get married?

(Have spouses share their answers with each other first. Then let a few volunteers "brag on" their spouses' qualities to the whole group.)

Applying the Principles
(10 minutes)

Have the group turn to the "Making It Work" section in the Participant's Guide.
Allow several minutes for people to work individually on their predictions. Then
let them discuss the results—as couples, not with the whole group.

As time allows, lead a whole-group discussion of questions like the following.

**Did you and your spouse agree on all your predictions? If not, what does
that tell you?**

(Chances are that spouses disagreed on some points. That suggests no spouse
is infallible, and that expectations should be taken with a grain of salt.)

Do we really know what to expect from our spouses? Why or why not?

(We all establish patterns over time, and tend to use our spouse's patterns to
predict and interpret behavior. The problem is that we also try to "prove" our assumptions about our mates by seeing everything they do as fitting the pattern. We
think we know what to expect, but that leaves out the possibility that a person
may do the unexpected.)

**Is it fair to assume what your spouse will do in a given situation? Why or
why not?**

(Sometimes it's prudent to assume that past behavior could be repeated—that
an abusive spouse might attack again, for example—and take precautions. Often,
though, we prejudge a mate and make a "preemptive strike" without knowing the
facts.)

**How could your expectations influence what your spouse actually does?
Is that good or bad?**

(Expecting the best of your spouse could lead him or her to "live up to" your expectations—a good thing. Expecting the worst could discourage a spouse from trying to change—a bad thing.)

If there are any expectations you'd be better off without, how will you get rid of them?

(It might help to ask your mate what he or she is thinking instead of assuming you know what's "really" on his or her mind; carefully observing actual behavior instead of just remembering patterns would be a reality check; next time an expectation causes you to feel angry or fearful, you could question its validity; asking God to help you give your spouse the same kind of "second chance" He's given you might be in order.)

6. BRINGING IT HOME

Reinforcing Your Point
(5 minutes)

Encourage couples to read the "Bringing It Home" section of their Participant's Guides during the week. The one corresponding to this session, written by a licensed counselor, explains how to be content with a spouse who's disappointed your expectations.

Here are some comments you might want to use in concluding your meeting.

In this session we've talked mostly about expectations that cause trouble. But I'd like to wrap up with an expectation that's worth holding on to. It can give us hope for our marriages—and the rest of our lives, too. It's from the Bible.

"Being confident of this, that he who began a good work in you will carry it on to completion until the day of Christ Jesus" (Philippians 1:6).

Has God been starting a good work in you during our times together? Have you picked up some advice you can use during the week? Can you see how you might be able to make a few "course corrections" in your marriage?

Just as marriage isn't "all about you," it isn't "all *up* to you," either. If God is part of your relationship, His power to follow through on what you're learning is available.

Close in prayer, thanking God that the couples in your group can expect His help as they work on making their marriages all they can be.

WALKING IN THEIR SHOES

What's it like to be your spouse? If that's beyond your powers of imagination, you'll find it hard to understand him or her.

Empathy—the ability to "feel for" and identify with someone else—goes a long way toward improving practically everything in a marriage, from communication to sex to spiritual closeness.

In this DVD segment, Gary Thomas notes that God's empathy for us is a model of how spouses should treat each other. Drs. Les and Leslie Parrott explain how our mates need more than our sympathy, how empathy creates safety, and how we can gain understanding by mentally "trading places" with our spouses.

Session Aim

To help group members practice empathizing with their spouses in order to better understand and support each other.

Setting the Stage

- Read this session plan and Chapter 6 in the Participant's Guide.
- Provide pencils or pens and sheets of paper (one per person).
- To prepare for the optional icebreaker in Step 1, bring half a dozen small paper bags, each containing a small object with a distinctive texture.
- Cue up the DVD to segment 6, "Walking in Their Shoes."

Optional Icebreaker
(5 minutes)

Here's a lighthearted way to start your session—if your group likes that sort of thing.

Before the meeting, find half a dozen small objects with distinctive textures (an unshelled peanut, a rubber eraser, a handful of dryer lint, etc.). Put each item in a small paper bag; fold the top of each bag so that the object can't be seen.

To start the session, hand each bag to a group member. Give the following instructions.

We're about to test your ability to "feel what someone else feels." If you've been given a paper bag, you should know there's an object inside. Don't let anyone see it. You'll take turns putting your hand in the bag and holding the object for 10 seconds. The rest of us will try to "feel what you're feeling" and write down what we think the item is.

Work your way through all the items. Then see who got the most objects right. Chances are that no one's score will be impressive.

Being able to "feel what someone else feels" doesn't usually involve paper bags. What word could be defined as "feeling what someone else feels"?

(Empathy.)

What kinds of people especially need empathy?

(Some group members may think of professions like pastoring, counseling, nursing, and acting. But the truth is that everybody needs it.)

Empathy isn't just for people who have certain jobs. Parents, for instance, need it to understand their children. And married people need it to understand and support their spouses.

Identifying Your Needs
(5-10 minutes)

Have group members turn to the "Finding Yourself" section in the Participant's Guide, where they'll see a survey designed to get them thinking about the session topic. Give them time to complete it, working individually. Then let volunteers share some results with the group.

1. **Which of the following do you think are good examples of empathy? Why?**
   ____ a near-stranger at church saying, "I know how you feel"
   ____ your mother baking you cookies when you're not invited to a party
   ____ President Bill Clinton saying, "I feel your pain"
   ____ your spouse giving you a back rub when you've had a hard day
   ____ Psalm 103:13-14
   ____ your dog staring dolefully at you when you're sad
   ____ other _____

   (Answers will vary, but the second, fourth, and fifth choices probably are better than the others.)

2. **On a scale of 1 to 10 (10 highest), how well do you think your spouse understands you in each of the following areas? How do you know?**
   ____ your fears
   ____ your dreams
   ____ your feelings about God
   ____ your feelings about work
   ____ your favorite dessert

   (If people are reluctant to answer this aloud, just have them think about it.)

3. **On a scale of 1 to 10 (10 highest), how well do you think you understand your spouse in each of the following areas? How do you know?**
   ____ his or her fears
   ____ his or her dreams
   ____ his or her feelings about God
   ____ his or her feelings about work
   ____ his or her favorite dessert

   (Answers will differ. The important thing here isn't the ratings, but to get participants to consider the effort they're putting into understanding their mate. Toward that end, ask whether group members *know* they understand their spouse, or whether they just *assume* they do.)

4. **What's one thing you've done in the last month to help you better understand your spouse?** _____

_____

(Some possibilities: Had a long talk; visited his or her workplace; reminisced with his or her parents; read something he or she had written.)

5. **If you haven't done anything, why is that? If you have, did it work? Why or why not?** _____

_____

(Replies will vary.)

3. CATCHING THE VISION

Watching and Discussing the DVD
(20-25 minutes)

After viewing the DVD, use questions like these to help couples think through the issues that were raised.

1. **How do you feel when you hear the following? Why?**
   - **"I know how you feel."**
   - **"You shouldn't feel that way."**
   - **"Tell me how you feel."**
   - **"My heart goes out to you."**
   - **"I can't imagine how you must feel."**

   (Responses will vary. Generally speaking, people don't appreciate it when others overstate their ability to empathize [sometimes true of the first example] or display a lack of empathy [as in the second]. Feelings about the other choices may depend on the relationship between the speaker and the hearer.)

2. **Gary Thomas points out that God understands us as no one else does. What difference does it make to you that God knows the following?**
   - **the number of hairs on your head**
   - **your thoughts**

- **how long you'll live**
- **the sins you've committed**
- **your prayers**
- **what you go through every day**

(Opinions will vary. Some may welcome God's knowledge of them, seeing it as a source of empathy; others may feel intimidated by His attention.)

3. **Which of the following do you think is most like God's empathy for you? Why? Which is most like the empathy one spouse needs to have for another?**
   - **the compassion a pet owner has for a dog or cat**
   - **the pity a passerby has for a homeless person**
   - **the protectiveness a parent has for a child**
   - **the understanding old friends have of each other**
   - **other** _____

(Opinions may vary, though it seems likely that God's empathy is most like the parent-child relationship. That wouldn't work in most marriages, though, where the understanding of old friends would be more appropriate.)

4. **Read Matthew 23:37 and Luke 23:32-35. How did Jesus show his empathy for people in these passages? Based on His example, how would you show understanding for your spouse in the following situations?**
   - **He or she learns of a close friend's sudden death.**
   - **He or she seems to be losing faith in God.**
   - **He or she lashes out verbally at you.**

(Jesus seemed to feel the lostness of Jerusalem's people, and wanted to guide and protect them; He knew His executioners didn't realize the significance of what they were doing, and forgave them. Following His example might mean "gathering" your spouse in a protective embrace, being patient with your spouse's skepticism, and forgiving a spouse who speaks angrily to you. [Note, however, that a pattern of verbal abuse in a marriage is a serious problem that must be addressed, often through counseling.])

5. **Drs. Les and Leslie Parrott say they'd like to give you a box containing the power of empathy. If there really were such a thing, how much do you**

think a one-month supply would cost? What would the packaging claim? What ingredients might be listed? What warnings about side effects might it include?

(Encourage people to come up with creative suggestions. Perhaps the manufacturer, in an effort to be empathetic, would have a sliding price scale—or maybe the price would be low because consumers aren't that interested in being sensitive to others. Packaging hype might promise the ability to read minds. Ingredients might include anything that enhances the ability to hear, see, or feel. Side effects might include a tendency to catch others' illnesses, or oversensitivity to bright lights and loud noises.)

6. **According to the Parrotts, how is empathy different from sympathy? Which one is "all heart," and which involves heart, mind, and action? How might the responses of a sympathetic spouse and an empathetic one differ in each of the following situations?**
    - **A husband dreads spending Thanksgiving with his in-laws, who've never approved of his "low-class" upbringing. How does the wife respond?**
    - **A wife has to go on a low-sugar diet due to diabetes. How does the husband respond?**
    - **A husband announces that he wants to become a policeman, even though his wife thinks it would be stressful and dangerous. How does the wife respond?**
    - **A wife is being overworked and underpaid by a clueless boss. How does the husband respond?**

(Sympathy may "feel for" another person, but empathy imagines itself in the other person's situation, better equipping the empathizer to take action. In the first example given, a sympathetic wife might tell her husband, "I'm sorry it's hard to be around my parents," while an empathetic wife might say, "If it happens again, I'll ask my parents to stop criticizing you." In the second situation, a sympathetic husband could say, "I'm sorry you have to give up desserts"; an empathetic one might give up desserts so that the wife won't be tempted by them. In the third case, a sympathetic wife might say, "I know you think being a policeman sounds exciting, but you have to put your family first"; an empathetic wife might express doubts but help the husband explore careers that meet his need for fulfillment and her need for security. In the last example, a sympathetic husband could express disgust and urge the wife to find a different job; an empathetic husband could see how things aren't that simple, and help his wife find ways to relieve the stress while looking for a long-term solution.)

7. **The Parrotts explain that empathy creates a safe, comfortable place for both spouses. What's one way in which your mate seems to understand you better than anyone else does? When does that mean the most to you?** (Answers will vary. If possible, be ready with a response from your own experience.)

8. **The Parrotts also advise that you need to understand yourself before you can understand your spouse. Which of the following best describes your reaction to that?**
    - **"I don't want to get in touch with my feelings."**
    - **"I'd rather do both at the same time."**
    - **"It makes sense, but I can't do it alone."**
    - **"My spouse has helped me understand myself."**
    - **other** _____

(Opinions may differ. If people find this question too personal, encourage them to just think about it.)

Bible Study
(10 minutes)

If your group makes Bible study a priority, have volunteers read some or all of these passages and discuss the questions that follow them.

> *Rejoice with those who rejoice; mourn with those who mourn. (Romans 12:15)*

1. **How would you follow this verse's principle in each of the following situations?**
    - **Your spouse just got home from a job you know he or she hates.**
    - **Your spouse just won an award you've never been able to win.**

- **You and your spouse are on the same diet; he or she gained three pounds this week, and you lost four.**

(Some possibilities: In the first case, you could avoid a chirpy, "So, how was work today?" In the second, you might send an "e-mail blast" to all your friends noting your spouse's achievement, even if you're a little jealous. In the third, you could avoid crowing about your weight loss and offer encouragement instead of "tips" gained from your "vast" experience.)

Like one who takes away a garment on a cold day, or like vinegar poured on soda, is one who sings songs to a heavy heart. (Proverbs 25:20)

2. **How does this verse provide a picture of empathy—or lack of it? If you're perky and optimistic and your spouse tends toward gloom and pessimism, how can you apply the wisdom of this proverb?**

(Answers will vary. This verse describes a sad person's reaction to being urged to "keep smiling"—musically or otherwise. An empathetic spouse realizes that a "negative" outlook isn't always wrong, and that calls for "positive" thinking aren't always welcome.)

If a man loudly blesses his neighbor early in the morning, it will be taken as a curse. (Proverbs 27:14)

3. **If one spouse is a "morning person" and the other is a "night owl," how can each show sensitivity to the other's needs? What if one is an extrovert and the other an introvert? What if one is a careful planner and the other likes to be spontaneous?**

(The answer usually isn't for one spouse to become more like the other. It's empathy—viewing the situation from your spouse's perspective rather than insisting that it change. That can lead to negotiating solutions that take both partners' needs into account.)

When Mary reached the place where Jesus was and saw him, she fell at his feet and said, "Lord, if you had been here, my brother would not have died."

When Jesus saw her weeping, and the Jews who had come along with her also weeping, he was deeply moved in spirit and troubled. "Where have you laid him?" he asked.

"Come and see, Lord," they replied.

Jesus wept.

Then the Jews said, "See how he loved him!" (John 11:32-36)

4. **Why did Jesus cry? Was it because He thought Lazarus was gone forever, or because He empathized with the grief of Mary and her friends?**

(Since Jesus knew that Lazarus was going to be raised from the dead, His tears probably reflected feeling the pain and helplessness His friends suffered.)

5. **From what you know of Jesus, would you say He really understands what it means to be human? If so, how did He get that understanding?**

(Some may wonder whether Jesus truly understands being a human spouse or parent. Still, as the Son of God, Christ is omniscient [knows all things]; as the Son of Man, He has the experience of "walking in our shoes." That combination is a powerful formula for empathy.)

6. **How does the experience of Jesus provide a model for someone who wants to better understand his or her spouse?**

(Here's how the apostle Paul put it in Philippians 2:5-7: "Your attitude should be the same as that of Christ Jesus: Who, being in very nature God, did not consider equality with God something to be grasped, but made himself nothing, taking the very nature of a servant, being made in human likeness." If Jesus was willing to walk in our shoes, we should be willing to walk in those of our spouse.)

Applying the Principles

(10 minutes)

Have the group turn to the "Making It Work" section in the Participant's Guide. Allow several minutes for individuals to complete the word-matching activity. Then ask them to discuss the results as couples.

If time allows, discuss as a whole group the following questions. Answers to the questions will vary; the point is to help spouses see things from the other person's point of view.

What's one thing you learned about your spouse from this exercise?

How could understanding and caring about that thing you learned make a difference in your relationship?

What words could you add to the first column that would reflect something you'd like to know about your spouse? Sometime during the week, add those words and do the exercise again.

Reinforcing Your Point
(5 minutes)

The Participant's Guide mentions one other idea couples can use during the week:

Here's another way to gain empathy with your spouse. Try writing your mate a letter in which you imagine what tomorrow will be like for him or her, including the three potentially most stressful times and how your spouse might feel about them. Then, if you like, pray together about those times and feelings.

Encourage group members to try that. Also encourage them to read the "Bringing It Home" section of their participant's guides later this week. They'll find advice from a counselor on how very different spouses can better understand each other.

Before closing with prayer, remind couples that when they need help to solve a marital problem, it's available from one or more Christian counselors in your area. If your church recommends one, provide contact information. Otherwise, participants may call Focus on the Family, which maintains a referral network of Christian counselors. For information, people can call 1-800-A-FAMILY and ask for the counseling department. They can also download free, printable brochures offering help for couples at http://www.focusonthefamily.com/marriage/articles/brochures.aspx.

About Our DVD Presenters
Essentials of Marriage: Higher Love

Stormie Omartian is a best-selling Christian author with more than eight million copies of her books *The Power of a Praying Wife, The Power of a Praying Parent, The Power of a Praying Husband, The Power of a Praying Woman,* and *The Power of Praying Together* in print. *The Power of a Praying Husband* received the Gold Medallion award in 2002. Currently living in Nashville, Stormie and her husband, Michael, have been married for over 25 years and have three children.

Dr. Les Parrott III is a professor of psychology and codirector with his wife, **Dr. Leslie Parrott**, of the Center for Relationship Development at Seattle Pacific University. He is a fellow in medical psychology at the University of Washington School of Medicine and an ordained minister in the Church of the Nazarene. Les earned his M.A. in theology and his Ph.D. in clinical psychology from Fuller Theological Seminary. Les has written more than 10 books, including *Questions Couples Ask, Becoming Soul Mates,* and *Saving Your Marriage Before It Starts* (all cowritten with Leslie).

Dr. Gary and Barb Rosberg, cofounders of America's Family Coaches, host a nationally syndicated daily radio program and have conducted conferences on marriage and family relationships in more than 100 cities across the country. The Rosbergs have written more than a dozen prominent marriage and family resources, including *The 5 Love Needs of Men & Women* (a Gold Medallion finalist) and *Divorce-Proof Your Marriage* (a Gold Medallion winner). Gary earned his Ed.D. from Drake University and has been a marriage and family counselor for more than 25 years. Married more than 30 years, the Rosbergs live outside Des Moines, Iowa, and have two married daughters and four grandchildren.

Dr. Greg Smalley earned his doctorate in clinical psychology from Rosemead School of Psychology at Biola University. He also holds master's degrees in counseling psychology (Denver Seminary) and clinical psychology (Rosemead School of Psychology). Greg is president of Smalley Marriage Institute, a marriage and family ministry in Branson, Missouri, and serves as chairman of the board of the National Marriage Association. Greg has published more than 100 articles on parenting and relationship issues. He is the coauthor of *The DNA of Parent-Teen Relationships* (with his father, Gary Smalley) and *The Men's Relational Toolbox* (with his father and his brother, Michael). Greg, his wife, Erin, and their three children live in Branson, Missouri.

Gary Thomas is a writer and the founder/director of the Center for Evangelical Spirituality, a speaking and writing ministry that combines Scripture, history, and the Christian classics. His books include *Sacred Marriage, Authentic Faith* (winner of the Gold Medallion award in 2003), and *Seeking the Face of God*. Gary has spoken in 49 states and four countries and has served as the campus pastor at Western Seminary, where he is an adjunct professor. Gary, his wife, Lisa, and their three kids live in Bellingham, Washington.

Mitch Temple is a licensed marriage and family therapist and author of *The Marriage Turnaround*. He holds two graduate degrees, in ministry and in marriage and family therapy, from Southern Christian University. Mitch currently serves as the director of the marriage department at Focus on the Family in Colorado Springs. He has conducted intensives nationwide for couples on the brink of divorce and has served as a family, pulpit, and counseling minister in churches for a total of 23 years. He was director of pastoral care, small groups, family ministry, and a counseling center at a large church for 13 years. He and his wife, Rhonda, have been married for more than 24 years and have three children.

Dr. Del Tackett is president of Focus on the Family Institute and senior vice president of Focus on the Family. He is also the architect and chief spokesperson for Focus on the Family's *The Truth Project*, a nationwide initiative designed to bring the Christian worldview to the body of Christ. He and his wife live in Colorado Springs, Colorado.

FOCUS ON THE FAMILY®

Welcome to the Family

Whether you purchased this book, borrowed it, or received it as a gift, we're glad you're reading it. It's just one of the many helpful, encouraging, and biblically based resources produced by Focus on the Family® for people in all stages of life.

Focus began in 1977 with the vision of one man, Dr. James Dobson, a licensed psychologist and author of numerous best-selling books on marriage, parenting, and family. Alarmed by the societal, political, and economic pressures that were threatening the existence of the American family, Dr. Dobson founded Focus on the Family with one employee and a once-a-week radio broadcast aired on 36 stations.

Now an international organization reaching millions of people daily, Focus on the Family is dedicated to preserving values and strengthening and encouraging families through the life-changing message of Jesus Christ.

Focus on the Family MAGAZINES

These faith-building, character-developing publications address the interests, issues, concerns, and challenges faced by every member of your family from preschool through the senior years.

| FOCUS ON THE FAMILY® MAGAZINE | FOCUS ON THE FAMILY CLUBHOUSE JR.® Ages 4 to 8 | FOCUS ON THE FAMILY CLUBHOUSE® Ages 8 to 12 | FOCUS ON THE FAMILY CITIZEN® U.S. news issues |

For More INFORMATION

ONLINE:

Log on to
FocusOnTheFamily.com
In Canada, log on to
FocusOnTheFamily.ca

PHONE:

Call toll-free:
800-A-FAMILY
(232-6459)
In Canada, call toll-free:
800-661-9800

Rev. 12/08

More Great Resources
from Focus on the Family®

Complete Guide to the First Five Years of Marriage: Launching a Lifelong, Successful Relationship

Thousands of couples have asked the counselors at Focus on the Family for insight into money, communication, and a host of other issues. Now their collective wisdom is available for you in this handy reference book, the *Complete Guide to the First Five Years of Marriage*. Hardcover.

Blueprints for a Solid Marriage
by Dr. Steve Stephens

Marriage, like a house, requires time, effort, and regular maintenance. Whether you are building the foundation, making repairs or needing to remodel your relationship, *Blueprints for a Solid Marriage* helps any time-strapped couple assess their relationship and then take action with an easy-to-follow plan and fun "marriage improvement projects." Hardcover.

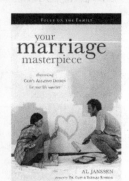

Your Marriage Masterpiece: Discovering God's Amazing Design for Your Life Together
by Al Janssen

Your Marriage Masterpiece takes a fresh look at the exquisite design God has for your marriage and brings to light the reasons your union was intended to last a lifetime. You will examine passion, adventure, commitment, and other principles that will make your marriage a masterpiece. And you will be reminded of God's love and passion for you and your spouse. Paperback.